BERNHARD ROETZEL

LOOK BOOK

h.f.ullmann

Ein Bild sagt mehr als tausend Worte. Als Autor müsste ich dieser Aussage widersprechen, denn mit tausend Worten kann man sehr viel mehr sagen. Wahr ist aber auch, dass Bilder für die Mode sehr wichtig sind. Ob es immer so war, lässt sich nicht belegen, doch seit der Antike kennen wir Darstellungen von Kleidung. Reisende Schneider verwendeten im 18. Jahrhundert Puppen, die nach der neuesten Mode gekleidet waren, damit sie der Kundschaft die neuen Trends schmackhaft machen konnten. Und ein Heer von Modeillustratoren war damit beschäftigt, die Seiten der Schneiderfachpresse, der Versandhauskataloge und der Zeitschriften zu füllen. Bis die Fotografie die Zeichnungen ablöste. Die digitale Bilderwelt hat die Kamera mit mechanischem Verschluss und Film längst abgelöst, der Hunger nach Bildern ist aber noch mehr gewachsen. Heute werden täglich Millionen von Fotos gemacht und in den sozialen Medien geteilt. Ein kleiner Teil davon zeigt klassische Kleidung. Auf Englisch heißt dieser Stil »permanent fashion«. So treffend die Bezeichnung klingt, so widersprüchlich ist sie. Mode lebt von Veränderung, der Freund des zeitlosen Stils liebt die Veränderung aber nicht. Dennoch gibt es nicht den einen klassischen Stil, das beweist dieses Buch. Den klassischen, zeitlosen Stil gibt es in einer so großen Zahl von Varianten, wie es Träger dieses Stils gibt.

A picture is worth a thousand words. Being a writer, I ought to contradict this adage, because there is so much more one can say with a thousand words. However, it is also true that pictures are extremely important in fashion. There is no way of proving whether this has always been the case, but we have known illustrations of clothing ever since classical antiquity. In the 18th century, travelling tailors used dolls dressed in the latest fashion to whet their clients' appetites for the newest trends. A whole army of fashion illustrators was kept busy to fill the pages of sartorial publications, of mail-order catalogs, and magazines. That was until photography took over from drawings. Nowadays, we have a world of digital pictures—no need, anymore, for mechanic shutters and film—and yet the thirst for images has even increased. These days, millions of photographs are being taken and shared on social media platforms every single day. A small part of these shows classic clothes in the style of what is nowadays called "permanent fashion." Although this term suggests a certain appropriateness it still is contradictory in itself, as fashion feeds on change but lovers of timeless style do not favour change. Yet, and this is what the book at hand will prove, there is no such thing as the classic style. Timeless, traditional style has as many variations as there are people who dress in this style.

FOREWORD ✕ **3**

BUSINESS GARDEROBE

In der klassischen Garderobe finden wir Anzüge aus dunkel-
blauem und dunkelgrauem Woll- oder Kaschmirtuch für das
Geschäft und abendliche Anlässe. Hellere Blau- und Grautöne,
eventuell dezent gemustert, für die Geschäftsreise oder weniger
förmliche Tagesanlässe. Außerdem Anzüge in Braun- und
Grüntönen, mit Muster oder einfarbig. Im Sommer kommen
Baumwoll-, Leinen und Seidenanzüge hinzu. Farbe und Stoff
sind nicht die einzigen Unterscheidungsmerkmale: Schnitt,
Passform und vor allem der Stil sind fast noch wichtiger.
Wie unterschiedlich Herren in ihren Anzügen wirken können
und was sie alles damit über sich aussagen, sehen wir
auf den folgenden Seiten.

BUSINESS WEAR

The traditional classic wardrobe includes suits made of dark blue or dark grey wool or cashmere fabric that can be worn both for daytime business and for evening events. Somewhat lighter blues and greys, maybe even with a very discreet pattern, are ideal for business travels and less formal daytime events. Also possible are suits in browns and greens, both patterned or plain. In summer, suits made of cotton, linen, or silk are added. Colour and fabric are not the only distinguishing criteria—what is equally, if not more, important is the cut, the fit, and the style. The following pages show how different the impression a gentleman makes can be, depending on what suits he wears, and what this tells us about him.

Maßanzug: Volkmar Arnulf.
Maßhemd: Camiceria Artigiana
Carmen. **Einstecktuch:** Eigenes
Design, gefertigt in Italien.
Grenadine-Krawatte nach Maß:
Neapolitanischer Krawattenmacher.
Brogues nach Maß: Jan Kielman.
**Laptop- und Aktentasche
nach Maß:** Hans Øster.

Bespoke suit: Volkmar Arnulf.
Bespoke shirt: Camiceria
Artigiana Carmen. Silk crepe
pocket square: Own design,
made in Italy. **Made-to-measure
grenadine tie:** Neapolitan
tiemaker. **Bespoke brogues:**
Jan Kielman. **Bespoke Laptop
folio and briefcase:** Hans Øster.

6 **TORSTEN
GRUNWALD**

Anzug: Gabo Napoli.
Maßhemd: Finamore 1925.
Leineneinstecktuch: Barba Napoli. **Oxfords:** Eduard Meier.
Aktentasche: Glenroyal.

Suit: Gabo Napoli. **Made-to-measure shirt:** Finamore 1925.
Linen **pocket square:** Barba Napoli. **Oxfords:** Eduard Meier.
Briefcase: Glenroyal.

Maßanzug: Sastrería Langa.
Maßhemd: Sastrería
Haberdashers. Handgemachte
Sieben-Falten-Krawatte:
TadinoStore. **Wolleinstecktuch:**
Massimo Dutti. **Uhr:** IWC Mark XVI.
Einzeln angefertigte **Oxfords:**
Lazo y Duque.

Made-to-measure suit: Sastrería
Langa. **Bespoke shirt:** Sastrería
Haberdashers. Handmade **seven-
fold tie:** TadinoStore. Wool **pocket
square:** Massimo Dutti. **Watch:**
IWC Mark XVI. Made-to-order
Oxfords: Lazo y Duque.

8 **SALVADOR
GODOY**

Maßanzug: Vaatturiliike Sauma.
Maßhemd: Luxire. Sechs-Falten-
Krawatte: Berg & Berg. **Ein-
stecktuch:** Rampley & Co.
Einzeln angefertigte **Oxfords:**
Vass. **Aktentasche:** Linjer.

Made-to-measure suit:
Vaatturiliike Sauma. **Bespoke
shirt:** Luxire. **Sixfold tie:** Berg &
Berg. **Pocket square:** Rampley &
Co. Made-to-order **Oxfords:**
Vass. **Briefcase:** Linjer.

Doppelreiher nach Maß aus
Wolle/Mohair: Kathrin Emmer.
Maßhemd: Gino Venturini.
Seidenschleife: John Comfort.
Rauleder-Oxfords nach Maß:
Larson & Jehan. **Strümpfe:**
Bresciani.

Bespoke suit made of wool and
mohair: Kathrin Emmer.
Bespoke shirt: Gino Venturini.
Silk bowtie: John Comfort.
Bespoke **suede oxfords:**
Larson & Jehan. **Socks:** Bresciani.

Maßanzug aus Solarostoff:
Eduardo de Simone. **Maßhemd:**
Fralbo. **Krawatte:** Serà Fine Silk.
Einstecktuch: Rubinacci.
Oxfords: Church's.
Sonnenbrille: Persol Steve
McQueen. **Uhr:** Tudor Black Bay.
Fahrrad: Scatto Italiano.

Bespoke Solaro **suit:** Eduardo de
Simone. **Bespoke shirt:** Fralbo.
Tie: Serà Fine Silk. **Pocket
square:** Rubinacci. **Oxfords:**
Church's. **Sunglasses:** Persol
Steve McQueen. **Watch:** Tudor
Black Bay. **Bike:** Scatto Italiano.

**GIORGIO
GIANGIULIO** ✕ **11**

Anzug: Cesare Attolini. **Hemd:** Cesare Attolini. **Krawatte** aus Kaschmir: Cesare Attolini. **Knopflochkette:** »Longevity« von The Armoury. **Strümpfe:** Sozzi Milano. **Loafer:** St. Crispin's.

Suit: Cesare Attolini. **Shirt:** Cesare Attolini. Cashmere **tie:** Cesare Attolini. **Lapel chain:** "Longevity" by The Armoury. **Socks:** Sozzi Milano. **Loafers:** St. Crispin's.

MICHAEL JONDRAL

Maßanzug: Mytailor.com. **Hemd:**
Fort Belvedere. **Krawatte** aus
Madder-Seide: Fort Belvedere.
Einstecktuch: Fort Belvedere.
Ungefütterte **Raulederhand-
schuhe:** Fort Belvedere.
Balmoralstiefel: Scarosso.
Schnürsenkel: Fort Belvedere.

Made-to-measure suit: Mytailor.
com. **Shirt:** Fort Belvedere.
Madder tie: Fort Belvedere. Silk
pocket square: Fort Belvedere.
Unlined suede **gloves:** Fort Belvedere. **Balmoral boots:** Scarosso.
Shoelaces: Fort Belvedere.

**SVEN RAPHAEL
SCHNEIDER** ✕ **13**

Doppelreiher nach Maß:
Tobias Tailors of Savile Row.
Maßhemd: Gino Venturini.
Krawatte: Tobias Tailors of
Savile Row. **Einstecktuch:**
Barba Napoli. **Oxford
Loafer:** Eduard Meier.

Bespoke suit: Tobias Tailors
of Savile Row. **Bespoke shirt:**
Gino Venturini. **Tie:** Tobias Tailors
of Savile Row. **Pocket square:**
Barba Napoli. **Oxford loafers:**
Eduard Meier.

14

**BERNHARD
ROETZEL**

Maßanzug: Sartoria Sodano.
Maßhemd: Vanacore. **Krawatte:**
Spacca Neapolis Ties. **Tassel-
loafer:** Herring Shoes.

Bespoke suit: Sartoria Sodano.
Bespoke shirt: Vanacore. **Tie:**
Spacca Neapolis Ties. **Tassel
loafers:** Herring Shoes.

NICOLA
RADANO 15

Einreiher nach Maß aus Stoff
von Reda: Kathrin Emmer.
Maßhemd: Gino Venturini.
Krawatte: Harvie & Hudson.
Boxcloth-**Hosenträger:** Albert
Thurston. **Fullstrap-Loafer:**
Eduard Meier.

Bespoke suit: Kathrin Emmer.
Bespoke shirt: Gino Venturini.
Tie: Harvie & Hudson. **Boxcloth
braces:** Albert Thurston.
Fullstrap loafers: Eduard Meier.

Tür bitte
schließen

× BERNHARD
ROETZEL

Maßanzug: Vaatturiliike Sauma.
Hemd: Berg & Berg. **Krawatte**
aus Shantungseide: Drake's
London. **Leineneinstecktuch:**
Kent Wang. Barathea-**Hosen-**
träger: Viola Milano. **Rauleder-**
Oxfords: Carmina. **Tasche:**
Linjer Soft Briefcase.

Made-to-measure suit:
Vaatturiliike Sauma. **Shirt:** Berg
& Berg. Shantung **silk tie:**
Drake's London. Linen **pocket**
square: Kent Wang. Barathea
braces: Viola Milano. **Suede**
oxfords: Carmina. **Bag:** Linjer
Soft Briefcase.

Dreiteiler nach Maß aus feiner Wolle: Sartoria Diletto. **Maßhemd:** Gino Venturini. **Seidenstrickbinder: Ascot. Einstecktuch:** Barba Napoli. **Strümpfe:** Bresciani. **Rauledertasselloafer:** Eduard Meier.

Bespoke three-piece **suit:** Sartoria Diletto. **Bespoke shirt:** Gino Venturini. Knitted **silk tie:** Ascot. **Pocket square:** Barba Napoli. **Socks:** Bresciani. Suede **tassel loafers:** Eduard Meier.

18 ✕ **BERNHARD ROETZEL**

Maßanzug: Vaatturiliike Sauma.
Maßhemd: Luxire. **Seiden-
krawatte:** Exquisite Trimmings.
Leineneinstecktuch: Viola
Milano. **Oxfords:** Alfred Sargent.
Aktentasche: Linjer.

Made-to-measure suit:
Vaatturiliike Sauma. **Made-to-
measure shirt:** Luxire. **Silk tie:**
Exquisite Trimmings. **Linen pocket
square:** Viola Milano. **Oxfords:**
Alfred Sargent. **Briefcase:** Linjer.

JUHO
REHAKKA 19

Doppelreiher nach Maß: Tobias Tailors of Savile Row. **Maßhemd:** Gino Venturini. **Seidenstrick-binder:** Ascot. **Einstecktuch:** Barba Napoli. **Rauledertassel-loafer:** Eduard Meier.

Bespoke suit: Tobias Tailors of Savile Row. **Bespoke shirt:** Gino Venturini. Knitted **silk tie:** Ascot. **Pocket square:** Barba Napoli. Suede **tassel loafers:** Eduard Meier.

BERNHARD ROETZEL

Maßanzug: Sartoria Sodano.
Maßhemd: Vanacore. **Krawatte:**
Spacca Neapolis Ties. **Rauleder-
Oxfords:** Barre & Brunel.

Bespoke suit: Sartoria Sodano.
Bespoke shirt: Vanacore.
Tie: Spacca Neapolis Ties.
Suede **oxfords:** Barre & Brunel.

NICOLA
RADANO

Maßanzug: Eduardo De Simone.
Maßhemd: Fralbo. **Krawatte:**
Vintage YSL. **Einstecktuch:** Serà
Fine Silk. Tassel **Loafer:** Barrett.
Uhr: Vintage Rolex Datejust 16013 .

Bespoke suit: Eduardo De Simone.
Bespoke shirt: Fralbo. **Tie:** Vintage
YSL. **Pocket square:** Serà Fine
Silk. Tassel **loafers:** Barrett. **Watch:**
Vintage Rolex Datejust 16013.

**GIORGIO
GIANGIULIO**

Eigens angefertigter **Anzug** aus
leichter Wolle: E-F-V. **Hemd:** Oscar
Jacobson. **Krawatte:** E. Marinella.
Oxfords: Herring »Edward II«.

Made-to-order light wool **suit**:
E-F-V. **Shirt:** Oscar Jacobson.
Silk **tie:** E. Marinella. **Oxfords:**
Herring "Edward II".

ERIK
MANNBY 23

Maßanzug: Zaremba Bespoke.
Maßhemd: Luca Avitabile.
Krawatte: Viola Milano.
Einstecktuch: Simonnot Godard.
Oxfords: Edward Green.

Bespoke suit: Zaremba Bespoke.
Bespoke shirt: Luca Avitabile.
Tie: Viola Milano. **Pocket square:**
Simonnot Godard. **Oxfords:**
Edward Green.

24 ╳ OLOF
NITHENIUS

Maßanzug: Tobias Tailors of Savile. **Maßhemd:** Emanuel Berg. **Krawatte:** Vanda Fine Clothing. **Leineneinstecktuch:** Barba Napoli. **Derby-Brogues:** Eduard Meier. **Tasche:** Hartmann Luggage.

Bespoke suit: Tobias Tailors of Savile Row. **Made-to-measure shirt:** Emanuel Berg. **Tie:** Vanda Fine Clothing. Linen **pocket square:** Barba Napoli. **Derby brogues:** Eduard Meier. **Bag:** Hartmann Luggage.

BERNHARD ROETZEL | 25

Maßsakko: Cesare Attolini.
Baumwollhosen: Cesare Attolini.
Hemd: Cesare Attolini. **Krawatte:**
Vintage von Cesare Attolini.
Einstecktuch aus Leinen:
Simonnot Godard. **Reverskette**
aus Koralle: Ascione Napoli.
Kniestrümpfe: Sozzi Milano.
Raulederloafer: Saint Crispin's.
Regenmantel: Vintage von
Mackintosh. **Handschuhe:** Meier
Bruecher. **Schal** aus Kaschmir und
Seide: Cesare Attolini. **Reisehut:**
James Lock.

Made-to-order jacket: Cesare
Attolini. Cotton **trousers:** Cesare
Attolini. **Shirt:** Cesare Attolini. **Tie:**
Vintage by Cesare Attolini. Linen
pocket square: Simonnot Godard.
Lapel chain made of coral:
Ascione Napoli **socks:** Sozzi Milano
Suede **loafer:** Saint Crispin's.
Raincoat: Vintage by Mackintosh.
Gloves: Meier Bruecher. Cashmere
and silk **scarf:** Cesare Attolini.
Traveller hat: James Lock.

MICHAEL JONDRAL
HERRENMODE

Cesare Attolini
Napoli

SAINT CRISPIN'S

Finamore 1925
Napoli

ORAZIO LUCIANO

FEDELI
MADE IN ITALY

SHOP ONLINE
WWW.MICHAELJONDRAL.COM

ÖFFNUNGSZEITEN:
MONTAG GESCHLOSSEN

SA 10-16 UHR

Blazer nach Maß: Michael Possanner. **Echtsilberknöpfe:** Eduard Meier. **Cavalrytwillhosen** nach Maß: Michael Possanner. **Maßhemd:** Gino Venturini. **Seidenkrawatte:** Tobias Tailors of Savile Row. **Einstecktuch** aus Leinen: Barba Napoli. Boxcloth-**Hosenträger:** Albert Thurston. **Oxfords:** Eduard Meier.

Bespoke blazer: Michael Possanner. Sterling silver **blazer buttons:** Eduard Meier. **Bespoke** cavalry twill **trousers:** Michael Possanner. **Bespoke shirt:** Gino Venturini. **Tie:** Tobias Tailors of Savile Row. Linen **pocket square:** Barba Napoli. **Boxcloth braces:** Albert Thurston. **Oxfords:** Eduard Meier.

Blazer nach Maß: Michael Possanner, Wien. **Blazerknöpfe** Echtsilber: Eduard Meier. **Maßhemd:** Gino Venturini. **Krawatte:** Spacca Neapolis Ties. **Einstecktuch:** Barba Napoli. **Cavalrytwill-Hosen:** Tobias Tailors of Savile Row. **Kniestrümpfe** aus feiner Wolle: Bresciani. **Oxfords nach Maß:** Vickermann & Stoya.

Bespoke blazer: Michael Possanner. Sterling silver **blazer buttons:** Eduard Meier. **Bespoke shirt:** Gino Venturini. **Tie:** Spacca Neapolis Ties. **Pocket square:** Barba Napoli. **Bespoke** cavalry twill **trousers:** Tobias Tailors of Savile Row. Fine woollen **socks:** Bresciani. **Bespoke oxfords:** Vickermann & Stoya.

Hopsack-**Maßsakko:** B&Tailor.
Hemd: Eton. **Krawatte:** Shibumi
Berlin. Fresko **Hosen nach Maß:**
Zaremba Bespoke. **Einstecktuch:**
R Culturi. **Flügelklappenschuhe:**
Yanko.

Bespoke hopsack **sports coat:**
B&Tailor. **Shirt:** Eton. **Tie:** Shibumi
Berlin. **Bespoke** fresco **trousers:**
Zaremba Bespoke. **Pocket
square:** R Culturi. **Wingtip
shoes:** Yanko.

Anzug: Vintage von A. Caraceni.
Hemd: Sangar. **Krawatte:** Vintage.
Knopflochblume: Miniatur-Nelke
von Fort Belvedere. **Einstecktuch**
mit handrollierter Kante: Fort Bel-
vedere. **Goldring** mit Tigerauge:
Vermeil. **Stiefel:** Trickers.
Schnürsenkel: Fort Belvedere.

Suit: Vintage by A. Caraceni. **Shirt:**
Sangar. **Tie:** Vintage. **Boutonnière:**
Mini carnation by Fort Belvedere.
Pocket square with hand-rolled
edges: Fort Belvedere. **Gold ring**
with Tiger's eye: Vermeil. **Boots:**
Trickers. **Laces:** Fort Belvedere.

Doppelreiher nach Maß aus
Stoff von Draper's: Kathrin Emmer.
Maßhemd: Gino Venturini.
Krawatte: Spacca Neapolis Ties.
Einstecktuch: Barba Napoli.
Rauleder-Tasselloafer:
Eduard Meier.

Bespoke suit of Draper's cloth:
Kathrin Emmer. **Bespoke shirt:**
Gino Venturini. **Tie:** Spacca.
Neapolis Ties **Pocket square:**
Barba Napoli. Suede **tassel
loafers:** Eduard Meier.

BERNHARD
ROETZEL

31

Maßkonfektionierter Einreiher
mit aufgesetzten Taschen: Belvest.
Maßhemd: Finamore 1925.
Krawatte: Hermès. **Einstecktuch:**
Barba Napoli. **Strümpfe:** Bresciani.
Rauledertasselloafer: Eduard Meier.

Made-to-measure suit with patch
pockets: Belvest. **Made-to-measure
shirt:** Finamore 1925. **Tie:** Hermès.
Pocket square: Barba Napoli.
Socks: Bresciani. Suede **tassel
loafers:** Eduard Meier.

32 **BERNHARD ROETZEL**

Anzug: Fields Tailoring. **Hemd:** Mangas. **Krawatte:** Ralph Lauren. **Einstecktuch:** Cencibel. **Oxfords:** Lottusse. **Strümpfe:** Urban. **Aktentasche:** Absolute Bretón.

Suit: Fields Tailoring. **Shirt:** Mangas. **Tie:** Ralph Lauren. **Pocket square:** Cencibel. **Oxfords:** Lottusse. **Socks:** Urban. **Briefcase:** Absolute Bretón.

DAVID GARCÍA BRAGADO 33

Maßanzug: Mytailor.com. **Hemd:** Fort Belvedere. **Strickkrawatte:** Fort Belvedere. **Knopflochblume:** Edelweiß von Fort Belvedere. **Einstecktuch** aus Madderseide mit handrollierter Kante: Fort Belvedere. **Taschenuhr:** Waltham. **Chukkaboots:** Allen-Edmonds.

Made-to-measure suit: Mytailor.com. **Shirt:** Fort Belvedere. Knitted silk **tie:** Fort Belvedere. **Boutonnière:** Edelweiss by Fort Belvedere. Silk **pocket square** with handrolled edges: Fort Belvedere. **Pocket Watch:** Waltham. **Chukka Boots:** Allen Edmonds.

SVEN RAPHAEL SCHNEIDER

Von Hand maßkonfektionierter
Seersuckeranzug: Cove & Co.
Maßhemd: Gino Venturini.
Seidenschleife: Blick Ties. **Knie-
strümpfe:** Bresciani. **Rauleder-
tasselloafer:** Eduard Meier.

Handmade **made-to-measure
suit:** Cove & Co. **Bespoke shirt:**
Gino Venturini. **Bow tie:** Blick Ties.
Socks: Bresciani. Suede **tassel
loafers:** Eduard Meier.

**BERNHARD
ROETZEL** ✕ **35**

Maßanzug: Sartoria Caracciolo.
Maßhemd: Vanacore. **Krawatte:**
Spacca Neapolis Ties. **Rauleder-**
Loafer: Herring Shoes.

Bespoke suit: Sartoria Caracciolo.
Bespoke shirt: Vanacore.
Tie: Spacca Neapolis Ties. Suede
loafers: Herring Shoes.

NICOLA
RADANO

Baumwollanzug nach Maß:
Baron & Earl. **Maßhemd:** Finamore
1925. **Krawatte** aus bedruckter
Seide: Drake's. **Einstecktuch:**
Barba Napoli. **Rauledertassel-
loafer:** Eduard Meier.

Made-to-measure cotton **suit:**
Baron & Earl. **Made-to-measure
shirt:** Finamore 1925. **Tie:** Drake's.
Pocket square: Barba Napoli.
Suede **tassel loafers:** Eduard
Meier.

BERNHARD
ROETZEL 37

Tweedweste nach Maß:
Schneiderarbeit aus Stoff von
Porter & Harding. Tweedhosen:
Schneiderarbeit aus Stoff von
Porter & Harding. Maßhemd:
Emanuel Berg. Manschetten-
knöpfe: Vintage. Strümpfe:
Falke. Penny-Loafer: George
Cleverley.

Bespoke tweed waistcoat:
Tailored with cloth by Porter &
Harding. Bespoke trousers:
Tailored with cloth by Porter &
Harding. Made-to-measure
shirt: Emanuel Berg. Cufflinks:
Vintage. Socks: Falke. Penny
loafers: George Cleverley.

WOLFGANG
HÖLKER

Anzug: Handgefertigt aus für Eduard Meier gewebtem Tweed. **Hemd:** Eduard Meier. **Krawatte:** Eduard Meier. **Rauleder-Tassel-loafer:** Eduard Meier.

Suit: handmade from tweed woven for Eduard Meier. **Shirt:** Eduard Meier. **Tie:** Eduard Meier. Suede **tassel loafer:** Eduard Meier.

PETER EDUARD MEIER 39

Maßanzug: Schneider aus Florenz. **Maßhemd:** Frank Foster. **Maßkrawatte** aus Wolle: Neapolitanische Werkstatt. **Seidensteck-tuch:** New & Lingwood. **Oxfords nach Maß:** Benjamin Klemann. **Schirm:** Anfertigung von James Smith & Sons. **Kaschmirschal:** Begg.

Bespoke suit: Tailor from Florence. **Bespoke shirt:** Frank Foster. **Bespoke wool tie:** Neapolitan tiemaker. Silk **pocket square:** New & Lingwood. **Bespoke oxfords:** Benjamin Klemann. **Umbrella:** Made-to-order at James Smith & Sons. Cashmere **scarf:** Begg.

TORSTEN GRUNWALD

Glencheckanzug nach Maß:
Tobias Tailors of Savile Row.
Maßhemd: Gino Venturini.
Krawatte: John Comfort.
Fullstraploafer aus Rauleder
von Eduard Meier. **Strümpfe:**
Bresciani.

Bespoke suit: Tobias Tailors of
Savile Row. **Bespoke shirt:** Gino
Venturini. **Tie:** John Comfort.
Suede **fullstrap loafer:** Eduard
Meier. **Socks:** Bresciani.

BERNHARD
ROETZEL 41

Anzug: Ring Jacket für
The Armoury. **Hemd:** Eton.
Krawatte: Shibumi Berlin.
Schirm: Fox Umbrellas.
Oxfords: Yanko.

Suit: Ring Jacket for The
Armoury. **Shirt:** Eton.
Tie: Shibumi Berlin.
Umbrella: Fox Umbrellas.
Oxfords: Yanko.

ANDREAS
WEINÅS

Maßanzug: John Coggin.
Maßhemd: Emanuel Berg.
Seidenstrickbinder: Drake's.
Einstecktuch: Barba Napoli.
Baumwollkniestrümpfe:
Von Jungfeld. Fullstraploafer:
Eduard Meier. Schirm: Maglia.

Bespoke suit: John Coggin.
Made-to-measure shirt:
Emanuel Berg. Knitted silk tie:
Drake's. Pocket square: Barba
Napoli. Socks: Von Jungfeld.
Fullstrap loafers: Eduard Meier.
Umbrella: Maglia.

BERNHARD
ROETZEL 43

Maßanzug: Mytailor.com.
Hemd mit Doppelmanschetten:
A. Caraceni. **Krawatte** aus
Madder-Seide: Fort Belvedere.
Knopflochblume: Edelweiß
von Fort Belvedere.
Seideneinstecktuch: Vintage.
Monkstrapschuhe:
Herringshoes. **Strümpfe:** Fort
Belvedere. **Ring:** 14 Karat Gold
mit dunkelgrünem Turmalin.

Made-to-measure suit: Mytailor.
com. **Shirt** with double cuffs:
A. Caraceni. Madder silk **tie:** Fort
Belvedere. **Bouttonière:**
Edelweiss by Fort Belvedere.
Silk **pocket square:** Vintage.
Monkstrap shoes: Herringshoes.
Socks: Fort Belvedere. **Ring:**
14 carat gold with dark green
Turmaline.

**SVEN RAPHAEL
SCHNEIDER**

Maßanzug: Gallo Tailoring.
Hemd: Mangas. **Krawatte:**
Cencibel. **Einstecktuch:** Cencibel.
Strümpfe: Urban. **Spectator-**
Schuhe: Vidal Fernandez Shoes.

Bespoke suit: Gallo Tailoring.
Shirt: Mangas. **Tie:** Cencibel.
Pocket square: Cencibel.
Socks: Urban. **Spectator shoes:**
Vidal Fernandez Shoes.

DAVID GARCÍA BRAGADO ⋉ 45

Hut: Christy's. **Kaschmirschal:** Dante. **Maßhemd:** Gino Venturini. **Wollkrawatte:** Wilh. Jungmann & Neffe. **Gabardinemantel:** Travellus von Ladage & Oelke. **Maßhosen** aus Cavalrytwill: Tobias Tailors. **Oxfords nach Maß:** Vickermann & Stoya.

Hat: Christy's. Cashmere **scarf:** Dante. **Bespoke shirt:** Gino Venturini. Wool **tie:** Wilh. Jungmann & Neffe. Gabardine **coat:** Travellus by Ladage & Oelke. **Bespoke cavalry twill trousers:** Tobias Tailors. **Bespoke oxfords:** Vickermann & Stoya.

BERNHARD ROETZEL

Hut: Borsalino. **Maßanzug:** Eduardo De Simone. **Mantel** nach Maß aus Vintage-Stoff: Alter Schneider aus Neapel. **Maßhemd:** Fralbo. **Krawatte:** Vintage YSL. **Tasselloafer:** Barrett. **Sonnenbrille:** Persol 3152. **Uhr:** Vintage Rolex Datejust 16013.

Hat: Borsalino. **Bespoke suit:** Eduardo De Simone. **Bespoke overcoat** made of vintage fabric: Old Neapolitan tailor. **Bespoke shirt:** Fralbo. **Tie:** Vintage YSL. **Tassel loafers:** Barrett. **Sunglasses:** Persol 3152. **Watch:** Vintage Rolex Datejust 16013.

Maßanzug: Vaatturiliike Sauma.
Maßhemd: Luxire. **Sieben-Falten-Krawatte:** Viola Milano.
Leineneinstecktuch: Simonnot Godard. **Hosenträger:** Drake's London. **Tassel-Loafer:** Septième Largeur. **Mappe:** Berg & Berg.

Made-to-measure suit: Vaatturiliike Sauma. **Made-to-measure shirt:** Luxire. **Seven-fold tie:** Viola Milano. Linen **pocket square:** Simonnot Godard. **Braces:** Drake's London. **Tassel loafers:** Septieme Largeur. **Portfolio:** Berg & Berg.

48 ✕ **JUHO REHAKKA**

Maßanzug: Tobias Tailors of Savile Row. **Maßhemd:** Gino Venturini. **Seidenstrickbinder:** Ascot. **Leineneinstecktuch:** Barba Napoli. **Hosenträger:** Albert Thurston. **Strümpfe:** Falke. **Fullstrap-Loafer:** Eduard Meier.

Bespoke suit: Tobias Tailors of Savile Row. **Bespoke shirt:** Gino Venturini. Knitted silk **tie:** Ascot. Linen **pocket square:** Barba Napoli. **Braces:** Albert Thurston. **Socks:** Falke. **Fullstrap loafers:** Eduard Meier.

Maßanzug: Mr Johnsons Wardrobe. **Rollkragenpullover:** Saman Amel. **Oxfords:** John Lobb.

Made-to-measure suit: Mr Johnson's wardrobe. **Turtleneck sweater:** Saman Amel. **Oxfords:** John Lobb.

50 ✕ **ANDREAS WEINÅS**

Maßanzug: Vaatturiliike Sauma.
Rollkragenpullover aus
Merinowolle: Berg & Berg.
Einstecktuch aus Wolle und
Seide: Drake's London. **Tassel-Loafer:** Septième Largeur.
Tasche: Linjer Soft Briefcase.

Made-to-measure suit:
Vaatturiliike Sauma. Merino wool
sweater: Berg & Berg. Wool and
silk **pocket square:** Drake's
London. **Tassel loafers:** Septième
Largeur. **Bag:** Linjer Soft Briefcase.

Mantel nach Maß: Sastrería Haberdashers. **Maßanzug:** Sastrería 91. **Maßhemd:** Sastrería Sánchez-Caro. Handgemachte **Sieben-Falten-Krawatte:** TadinoStore. **Seideneinstecktuch:** TadinoStore. Einzeln angefertigte **Oxfords:** Lazo y Duque.

Made-to-measure covercoat: Sastrería Haberdashers. **Bespoke suit:** Sastrería 91. **Bespoke shirt:** Sastrería Sánchez-Caro. Handmade **sevenfold tie:** TadinoStore. **Pocket square:** TadinoStore. Made-to-order **oxfords:** Lazo y Duque.

52 SALVADOR GODOY

Trenchcoat: Eduard Meier.
Maßanzug: Kathrin Emmer.
Maßhemd: Gino Venturini.
Krawatte: Harvie & Hudson.
Strümpfe: Bresciani. **Fullstrap-Loafer:** Eduard Meier.

Trenchcoat: Eduard Meier.
Bespoke suit: Kathrin Emmer.
Bespoke shirt: Gino Venturini.
Tie: Harvie & Hudson. **Socks:** Bresciani. **Fullstrap loafers:** Eduard Meier.

Handgemachter **Maßanzug:**
Cove & Co. **Maßhemd:** Gino
Venturini. **Krawatte:** Turnbull &
Asser. **Leineneinstecktuch:**
Barba Napoli. **Strümpfe:**
Bresciani. **Oxford-Loafers:**
Eduard Meier.

Handmade **made-to-measure
suit:** Cove & Co. **Bespoke shirt:**
Gino Venturini. **Tie:** Turnbull &
Asser. Linen **pocket square:**
Barba Napoli. **Socks:** Bresciani.
Oxford loafers: Eduard Meier.

Hut: Roeckl. **Anzug:** Vintage von A. Caraceni. **Weste:** Mytailor.com. **Taschenuhr:** Gruen Verithin. **Hemd:** Vintage von Giovanni Verale. **Krawatte:** Vintage. **Knopflochblume:** Weißer Flachs von Fort Belvedere. **Einstecktuch mit handrollierter Kante:** Fort Belvedere. **Spectator-Schuhe:** Allen Edmonds.

Hat: Roeckl. **Suit:** Vintage by A. Caraceni. **Waistcoat:** Mytailor.com. **Pocket watch:** Gruen Verithin. **Shirt:** Vintage by Giovanni Verale. **Tie:** Vintage. **Bouttonière:** White Phlox by Fort Belvedere. Wool **pocket square:** Fort Belvedere. **Spectator shoes:** Allen Edmonds.

WOCHENENDE COUNTRY STYLE

Die englische Bekleidungstradition teilt die Garderobe in Stadt- und Landkleidung ein. Wobei das Wochenende in der Stadt als Einbruch des Landlebens in die urbane Umgebung zu verstehen ist. Am Wochenende kleidet sich der Städter wie bei einem wirklichen Landaufenthalt. »Land« im Sinne der klassischen Kleidung verbindet man mit Jagd, Reiten, Angeln, Spaziergänge oder vielleicht auch mit der Aquarellmalerei. Was man sich eben unter den ländlichen Beschäftigungen der britischen Oberklasse vorstellt. Die klassische Kleidung des Wochenendes orientiert sich stilistisch außerdem an den Dresscodes des amerikanischen Yvy-League-Stils und bayerisch-österreichischen Einflüssen.

WEEKEND COUNTRY STYLE

Traditionally, in the UK a distinction is made between ward-robe for the city and for the countryside. Having said that, a weekend spent in the city is usually seen as country life transported to urban surroundings. At the weekend, even city dwellers dress as if they were heading for a proper stay in the countryside. With reference to classic clothes, the "country look" is associated with pastimes such as shooting, riding, fishing, walking, and maybe even water-colour painting. In short, anything that you would imagine the British upper classes to be doing when they reside in the countryside. The weekend wear of classic style has furthermore been influenced by the style of American Ivy-League outfits and by the Bavarian-Austrian look.

Handgemachtes **Tweedsakko:**
Eduard Meier. **Maßhemd:** Gino
Venturini. **Strickweste** aus Lamm-
wolle: Alan Paine. **Wollkrawatte:**
Wilh. Jungmann & Neffe. **Ein-
stecktuch:** Barba Napoli. **Oxfords
nach Maß:** Vickermann & Stoya.
Kniestrümpfe aus feiner Wolle:
Sorley Socks.

Handmade **tweed jacket:**
Eduard Meier. **Bespoke shirt:**
Gino Venturini. Knitted lambswool
waistcoat: Alan Paine. Wool **tie:**
Wilh. Jungmann & Neffe. **Pocket
square:** Barba Napoli. **Bespoke
oxfords:** Vickermann & Stoya. Fine
woollen **socks:** Sorley Socks.

BERNHARD
ROETZEL

Flanellsakko: Vintage von A. Caraceni. **Hemd:** Vintage von Siniscalchi. **Krawatte:** Fort Belvedere. **Einstecktuch** mit handrollierten Kanten: Fort Belvedere. **Maßhosen** aus Baumwolltwill: Kiito bespoke tailor. **Strümpfe:** Fort Belvedere. **Double-Monkstrapschuhe:** Shoepassion.

Flannel **jacket:** Vintage by A. Caraceni. **Shirt:** Vintage by Siniscalchi. **Tie:** Fort Belvedere. **Pocket square** with hand-rolled edges: Fort Belvedere. **Bespoke cotton twill pants:** Kiito bespoke tailor. **Socks:** Fort Belvedere. **Double monkstrap shoes:** Shoepassion.

Maßsakko: Sartoria Crimi.
Kordhosen nach Maß: Sartoria
Ripense. **Lodenmantel:** Vintage,
vom Großvater. **Fedora-Hut:**
Borsalino. **Denimhemd:** American
Apparel. Japanisches **Bandana-
Tuch:** Kapital. **Strümpfe:**
Bresciani. **Norweger:** Crockett
& Jones. **Uhr:** Omega aus den
1950ern mit Maßarmband von
l'atelier du bracelet parisien.

Bespoke jacket: Sartoria Crimi.
Bespoke corduroy **trousers:**
Sartoria Ripense. **Overcoat:**
Grandfather Vintage Loden.
Fedora hat: Borsalino. Denim
shirt: American Apparel. Japanese
cotton **bandana:** Kapital.
Socks: Bresciani. **Norwegian
aproned derby:** Crockett &
Jones. **Watch:** 1950s vintage
Omega with bespoke strap from
l'atelier du bracelet parisien.

STÉPHANE
BUTTICÉ

Maßanzug aus Thornproof-Tweed: Tobias Tailors of Savile Row. **Maßhemd:** Emanuel Berg. **Wollkrawatte:** John Kent. **Einstecktuch:** Vintage, unbekannter Hersteller. **Derby-Schuhe:** Eduard Meier. **Hut:** Herbert Johnson.

Bespoke thornproof **tweed suit:** Tobias Tailors of Savile Row. **Made-to-measure shirt:** Emanuel Berg. Wool **tie:** John Kent. **Pocket square:** Vintage, unknown brand. **Derby shoes:** Eduard Meier. **Hat:** Herbert Johnson.

Sakko aus Wolle und Leinen:
SuitSupply. **Baumwollhosen**
nach Maß: Luxire. **Maßhemd:**
Luxire. **Krawatte:** Berg & Berg
Baumwolleinstecktuch:
Drake's London. **Hosenträger:**
Vaatturiliike Sauma. **Rauleder-**
Fullstrap-Loafer: Septième
Largeur. **Tasche:** Mismo.

Wool linen blend **jacket:**
SuitSupply. **Made-to-measure**
cotton **trousers:** Luxire.
Made-to-measure shirt: Luxire.
Tie: Berg & Berg. Cotton **pocket**
square: Drake's London.
Braces: Vaatturiliike Sauma.
Suede **fullstrap loafers:**
Septième Largeur. **Bag:** Mismo.

 **JUHO**
REHAKKA

Hopsack-Maßsakko: Sartoria CorCos. **Maßhosen** aus Kammgarnstoff: Zaremba bespoke. **Maßhemd:** Luca Avitabile. **Krawatte** aus Macclesfield-Seide: H. N. White. **Einstecktuch:** Simonnot Godard. **Oxfords:** Allen Edmonds.

Bespoke Hopsack **jacket:** Sartoria CorCos. **Bespoke** worsted **trousers:** Zaremba bespoke. **Bespoke shirt:** Luca Avitabile. Macclesfield silk **tie:** H. N. White. **Pocket square:** Simonnot Godard. **Oxfords:** Allen Edmonds.

Maßjacke aus Harris-Tweed: Sartoria Caliendo. **Strickjacke** aus Lammwolle: Anderson & Sheppard. **Jeans nach Maß** aus japanischem Denim: Levi's. **Kaschmireinstecktuch:** Anderson & Sheppard. **Stiefel:** Edward Green.

Bespoke Harris **tweed jacket**: Sartoria Caliendo. **Bespoke** Japanese-denim **jeans**: Levi's. Lambswool **cardigan:** Anderson & Sheppard. Cashmere **pocket square:** Anderson & Sheppard. **Boots:** Edward Green.

Tweedsakko nach Maß: Tobias Tailors of Savile Row. **Maßhemd:** Emanuel Berg. **Wollstrickbinder:** Ascot. **Einstecktuch:** Vintage, unbekannter Hersteller. **Wollstrümpfe:** Eduard Meier. **Derby-Schuhe:** Eduard Meier. **Filzhut:** Christy's. **Sitzstock:** Akah Lederwaren.

Bespoke tweed jacket: Tobias Tailors of Savile Row. **Made-to-measure shirt:** Emanuel Berg. Emanuel Berg. Knitted wool **tie:** Ascot. **Pocket square:** Vintage, unknown brand. **Socks:** Eduard Meier. **Derby shoes:** Eduard Meier. **Hat:** Christy's. **Folding walking stick seat:** Akah Lederwaren.

Handgemachtes **Tweedsakko:** Eduard Meier. **Maßhemd:** Gino Venturini. **Krawatte:** Eduard Meier. **Kordhosen:** Cordings of Piccadilly. **Strümpfe:** Falke. **Brogues:** Eduard Meier.

Handmade tweed jacket: Eduard Meier. **Bespoke shirt:** Gino Venturini. **Tie:** Eduard Meier. **Corduroys:** Cordings of Piccadilly. **Socks:** Falke. **Brogues:** Eduard Meier.

BERNHARD ROETZEL

Maßsakko: Sartoria Sodano.
Maßhosen: Sartoria Sodano.
Hemd: Vanacore. **Krawatte:**
Spacca Neapolis Ties. **Rauleder-
Loafer:** Herring Shoes.

Bespoke jacket: Sartoria Sodano.
Bespoke trousers: Sartoria So-
dano. **Bespoke shirt:** Vanacore.
Tie: Spacca Neapolis Ties.
Suede **loafers:** Herring Shoes.

NICOLA
RADANO 67

Sommersakko nach Maß: Sartoria Caliendo. **Leinenhemd** nach Maß: Luca Avitabile. **Krawatte:** Mattabisch für The Armoury. **Leinenhosen:** Paul Stuart. **Rauleder-Loafer nach Maß:** Stefano Bemer.

Bespoke jacket: Sartoria Caliendo. **Bespoke** linen **shirt:** Luca Avitabile. **Tie:** Mattabisch for The Armoury. Linen **trousers:** Paul Stuart. **Bespoke** suede **loafers:** Stefano Bemer.

Tweedjacke: Eduard Meier.
Hemd: Braun Hamburg.
Wollkrawatte: Spacca Neapolis
Ties. **Kordhosen:** Cordings of
Piccadilly. **Strümpfe:** Sorley
Socks. **Brogues:** Eduard Meier.

Tweed jacket: Eduard Meier.
Shirt: Braun Hamburg.
Wool **tie:** Spacca Neapolis Ties.
Corduroy **trousers:** Cordings of
Piccadilly. **Socks:** Sorley Socks.
Brogues: Eduard Meier.

BERNHARD
ROETZEL 69

Maßsakko: Olego Tailoring.
Hemd: Mangas. **Krawatte:**
Cencibel. **Einstecktuch:** Cencibel.
Hosen: Olego Tailoring.
Strümpfe: Urban. **Rauleder-
Tasselloafer:** Vidal Fernandez.

Bespoke jacket: Olego Tailoring.
Shirt: Mangas. **Tie:** Cencibel.
Pocket square: Cencibel.
Trousers: Olego Tailoring. **Socks:**
Urban. Suede **tassel loafers:**
Vidal Fernandez.

70 DAVID GARCÍA
BRAGADO

Sakko: Vintage von A. Caraceni.
Sonnenbrille: Acetate von Lafont.
Hemd: Vintage von Siniscalchi.
Krawatte aus Madder-Seide: Fort
Belvedere. **Krawattenklammer:**
Tigerauge, vintage. **Goldring** mit
Tigerauge: Vermeil. **Mini Nelke:**
Fort Belvedere. **Einstecktuch** mit
handrollierter Kante: Fort Belvedere.
Hosen: Vintage von A. Caraceni.
Monkstrap-Schuhe: Shoepassion.

Jacket: Vintage by A. Caraceni.
Sunglasses: Acetate by Lafont.
Shirt: Vintage by Siniscalchi.
Madder silk **tie:** Fort Belvedere.
Tie bar: Tiger's eye, vintage.
Gold ring with Tiger's eye: Vermeil.
Bouttonière: White Carnation by
Fort Belvedere. **Pocket square**
with hand rolled edges: Fort
Belvedere. **Trousers:** Vintage by
A. Caraceni. **Monkstrap shoes:**
Shoepassion.

Kordjacke: J. Keydge.
Maßhemd: Gino Venturini.
Strickweste: Alan Paine.
Seidentuch: Turnbull & Asser.
Chinos: Land's End.
Strümpfe: Eduard Meier.
Rauleder **Fullstrap-Loafer:**
Eduard Meier.

Corduroy **jacket:** J. Keydge.
Bespoke shirt: Gino Venturini.
Knitted **waistcoat:** Alan Paine.
Silk **square:** Turnbull & Asser.
Chinos: Land's End. **Socks:**
Eduard Meier. Suede **fullstrap
loafers:** Eduard Meier.

72 **BERNHARD
ROETZEL**

Raulederjacke nach Maß: Stòffa.
Rollkragenpullover: Ströms.
Jeans: Chad Prom. **Sneakers:**
CQP. **Raulederaktentasche:**
László Vass.

Made-to-measure suede
jacket: Stòffa. **Turtleneck**
sweater: Ströms. **Jeans:** Chad
Prom. **Sneakers:** CQP. Suede
briefcase: Laszlo Vass.

Maßsakko aus Wolle und Kaschmir: Sartoria Solito. **Maßhosen** aus altem Kavallerie-Twill: Sartoria CorCos. **Maßhemd** aus Oxfordstoff: Francesco Merolla. **Krawatte** aus Seidengrenadine: Viola Milano. **Seideneinstecktuch:** Viola Milano. **Oxfords:** Edward Green.

Bespoke jacket of wool and cashmere fabric: Sartoria Solito. **Bespoke trousers** made of vintage cavalry twill: Sartoria CorCos. **Bespoke shirt** made of Oxford cloth: Francesco Merolla. Silk Grenadine **tie:** Viola Milano. Silk **pocket square:** Viola Milano. **Oxfords:** Edward Green.

OLOF NITHENIUS

Handgemachtes **Tweedsakko:**
Eduard Meier. **Maßhemd:**
Emanuel Berg. **Wollstrickbinder:**
Ascot. **Einstecktuch:** Vintage,
unbekannter Hersteller. **Kord-
hosen:** Chelsea Farmer's Club.
Wollstrümpfe: Eduard Meier.
Derby-Schuhe: Eduard Meier.

Handmade **tweed jacket:** Eduard
Meier. **Made-to-measure shirt:**
Emanuel Berg. Knitted wool **tie:**
Ascot. **Pocket square:** Vintage,
unknown brand. **Corduroys:**
Chelsea Farmer's Club. **Socks:**
Eduard Meier. **Derby shoes:**
Eduard Meier.

Maßweste: Olego Tailoring.
Hemd: Massimo Dutti.
Maßhosen: Olego Tailoring.
Socken: Urban. **Rauleder-
Oxfords:** Vass Shoes.

Bespoke waistcoat: Olego
Tailoring. **Shirt:** Massimo Dutti.
Trousers: Olego Tailoring.
Socks: Urban. Suede **oxfords:**
Vass Shoes.

76

DAVID GARCÍA
BRAGADO

Lodenweste: Eduard Meier.
Wollpullover: Unbekannter englischer Hersteller. **Maßhemd**: Emanuel Berg. **Moleskinhosen:** Daniels & Korff. **Wollstrümpfe:** Eduard Meier. **Derby-Schuhe:** Eduard Meier.

Loden **waistcoat:** Eduard Meier. Wool **sweater:** Unkown English maker. **Made-to-measure shirt:** Emanuel Berg. **Moleskin trousers:** Daniels & Korff. **Socks:** Eduard Meier. **Derby shoes:** Eduard Meier.

BERNHARD ROETZEL 77

Jägerleinenjacke mit Loden-
kragen: Eduard Meier. **Maßhemd:**
Gino Venturini. **Krawattenschal:**
John Comfort. **Hosen** aus Leinen
und Baumwolle: Purwin &
Radczun. **Strümpfe:** Falke.
Fullstrap-Loafer: Eduard Meier.

Linen **jacket** with loden collar:
Eduard Meier. **Bespoke shirt:**
Gino Venturini. Silk **scarf:**
John Comfort. Cotton and linen
trousers: Purwin & Radczun.
Socks: Falke. **Fullstrap
loafers:** Eduard Meier.

**BERNHARD
ROETZEL**

Maßsakko: Sartoria Peluso.
Maßhosen: Sartoria Ripense.
Rollkragenpullover: William Lockie. **Wolleinstecktuch:** Calabrese 1924. **Strümpfe:** Di Carlo. **Chukkaboots:** Antica Cuoieria Firenze.

Bespoke jacket: Sartoria Peluso. **Bespoke trousers:** Sartoria Ripense. **Turtleneck sweater:** William Lockie. Wool **pocket square:** Calabrese 1924. **Socks:** Di Carlo. **Chukka boots:** Antica Cuoieria Firenze.

Tweedjacke: Eduard Meier.
Maßhemd: Gino Venturini.
Weste: Vintage, englisch.
Seidenbinder: Striessnig.
Kordhosen: Brooks Taverner.
Chukkaboots: Eduard Meier.

Tweed jacket: Eduard Meier.
Bespoke shirt: Gino Venturini.
Waistcoat: Vintage, English.
Tie: Striessnig. Corduroy
trousers: Brooks Taverner.
Chukka boots: Eduard Meier.

BERNHARD
ROETZEL

Kappe aus Harris Tweed: Miler
Menswear. Rollkragenpullover
aus Seide und Wolle: Massimo
Dutti. Eigens angefertigter
Safariblazer aus Wolle: E-F-V.
Flanellhosen: Oscar Jacobson.
Stiefel: Loake »Hyde«.

Harris Tweed newsboy cap:
Miler Menswear. Silk/wool
turtleneck sweater: Massimo
Dutti. Made-to-order wool Safari
blazer: E-F-V. Flannel trousers:
Oscar Jacobson. Boots: Loake
"Hyde".

ERIK
MANNBY 81

Filzhut: Brixton. Eigens ange-
fertigter **Flanellblazer:** E-F-V.
Maßhemd: Shirtonomy. **Seiden-
stickbinder:** Herrainpukimo.
Strickjacke: J. Lindeberg.
Baumwollhosen nach Maß:
Luxire. **Derby-Schuhe:** Church's
»Shannon«.

Felt hat: Brixton. Made-to-order
flannel **blazer:** E-F-V. **Made-to-
measure shirt:** Shirtonomy. Knitted silk **tie:** Herrainpukimo. Wool
cardigan: J. Lindeberg. **Made-
to-measure** cotton **trousers:**
Luxire. **Derby shoes:** Church's
"Shannon".

ERIK
MANNBY

Maßsakko: Olego Tailoring.
Hemd: Mangas. **Krawatte:**
Cencibel. **Einstecktuch:** Cencibel.
Hosen: Olego Tailoring.
Strümpfe: Urban. **Tassel-Loafer:**
Vidal Fernandez.

Bespoke jacket: Olego Tailoring.
Shirt: Mangas. **Tie:** Cencibel.
Pocket square: Cencibel.
Trousers: Olego Tailoring.
Socks: Urban. **Tassel loafers:**
Vidal Fernandez.

Jacke: Harry Stedman. **Hemd:** Harry Stedman. **Hosen:** Harry Stedman. **Derby-Brogues:** G. H. Bass. **Sonnenbrille:** Oliver Peoples.

Jacket: Harry Stedman. **Shirt:** Harry Stedman. **Trousers:** Harry Stedman. **Derby brogues:** G. H. Bass. **Sunglasses:** Oliver Peoples.

84 ✕ DAVID EVANS

Blazer mit aufgesetzten Taschen:
Belvest. **Maßhemd:** Emanuel
Berg. **Seidenstrickbinder:** Ascot.
Strickweste aus Lammwolle:
Alan Paine. **Kordhosen:** Cordings
of Piccadilly. **Wollstrümpfe:**
Eduard Meier. Rauleder **Fullstrap-
Loafer:** Eduard Meier.

Blazer with patch pockets:
Belvest. **Made-to-measure shirt:**
Emanuel Berg. Knitted silk **tie:**
Ascot. Knitted lambswool **waist-
coat:** Alan Paine. **Corduroys:**
Cordings of Piccadilly. **Socks:**
Eduard Meier. Suede **fullstrap
loafers:** Eduard Meier.

Lederjacke: Stewart. **Maßhemd:** Fralbo. **Maßjeans:** Marco Cerrato Napoli. **Stiefel:** Vintage Red Wing 875. **Sonnenbrille:** Persol 649. **Uhr:** Tudor Black Bay.

Leather jacket: Stewart. **Bespoke shirt:** Fralbo. **Bespoke jeans:** Marco Cerrato Napoli. **Boots:** Vintage Red Wing 875. **Sunglasses:** Persol 649. **Watch:** Tudor Black Bay .

GIORGIO GIANGIULIO

Büffellederjacke: El Corte Inglés. Baumwoll und **Kaschmirpullover:** Cortefiel. **Baumwollhosen** nach Maß: Sastrería Haberdashers. Einzeln angefertigte **Chukka-Boots:** Vidal Fernández.

Buffalo **leather jacket:** El Corte Inglés. Cotton and cashmere **jersey:** Cortefiel. **Made-to-measure** cotton **trousers:** Sastrería Haberdashers. Made-to-order **Chukka boots:** Vidal Fernández.

SALVADOR GODOY 87

Maßsakko aus Shetlandwolle: Eduardo De Simone. **Maßhemd:** Fralbo. **Flanellhosen** nach Maß: Marco Cerrato. **Krawatte:** Nicky Milano. **Einstecktuch:** Rubinacci. **Oxfords:** Custom Church's Diplomat. **Sonnenbrille:** Persol 649. **Uhr:** Tudor Black Bay.

Bespoke Shetland **jacket:** Eduardo De Simone. **Bespoke shirt:** Fralbo. **Bespoke** flannel **trousers:** Marco Cerrato. **Tie:** Nicky Milano. **Pocket square:** Rubinacci. **Oxfords:** Custom Church's Diplomat. **Sunglasses:** Persol 649. **Watch:** Tudor Black Bay.

GIORGIO GIANGIULIO

Handgemachtes **Tweedsakko:**
Eduard Meier. **Maßhemd:** Gino
Venturini. **Krawatte:** Cordings of
Piccadilly **Einstecktuch:** Vintage
unbekannter Marke. **Kordhosen:**
Brooks Taverner. **Kniestrümpfe:**
Falke. **Brogues:** Eduard Meier.

Handmade **tweed jacket:** Eduard
Meier. **Bespoke shirt:** Gino
Venturini. **Tie:** Cordings of
Piccadilly **Pocket square:** Vinta-
ge, unknown brand. **Corduroys:**
Brooks Taverner. **Socks:** Falke.
Brogues: Eduard Meier.

Maßblazer: d' Avenza.
Maßhemd: Gino Venturini.
Krawatte: Polo Ralph Lauren.
Leineneinstecktuch: Barba
Napoli. **Chinos:** Land's End.
Strümpfe: Falke. **Rauleder-
Tassel-Loafer:** Eduard Meier.
Reisetasche: Hartmann Luggage.

Made-to-measure blazer:
d' Avenza. **Bespoke shirt:** Gino
Venturini. **Tie:** Polo Ralph Lauren.
Linen **pocket square:** Barba
Napoli. **Chinos:** Land's End.
Socks: Falke. Suede **tassel
loafers:** Eduard Meier. **Overnight
bag:** Hartmann Luggage.

90 ✕ **BERNHARD
ROETZEL**

Baumwolljacke: Boglioli.
Baumwollhosen nach Maß:
Sartoria CorCos. **Maßhemd** aus
Oxfordstoff: Francesco Merolla.
Einstecktuch: Viola Milano.
Raulederbrogues: Loake 1880.

Cotton **jacket:** Boglioli: **Bespoke**
cotton **trousers:** Sartoria CorCos.
Bespoke shirt made of Oxford
cloth: Francesco Merolla.
Pocket square: Viola Milano.
Suede **brogues:** Loake 1880.

OLOF
NITHENIUS 91

Maßjacke: Sastrería Haberdashers.
Polohemd nach Maß aus Denim:
Sastrería Haberdashers. **Baum-
wollhosen** nach Maß: Sastrería
Haberdashers. Handgemachte
Sieben-Falten-Krawatte: Tadino-
Store. **Einstecktuch:** TadinoStore.
Einzeln angefertigte **Penny loafer:**
Vidal Fernández.

Made-to-measure jacket:
Sastrería Haberdashers. **Made-
to-measure** denim **polo shirt:**
Sastrería Haberdashers. **Made-
to-measure** cotton **trousers:**
Sastrería Haberdashers. Hand-made
sevenfold tie: TadinoStore.
Pocket square: TadinoStore.
Made-to-order **Penny loafers:**
Vidal Fernández.

**SALVADOR
GODOY**

Moleskinjacke: Eduard Meier.
Maßhemd: Gino Venturini.
Pullunder aus Lammwolle: John
Crocket. **Wollstrümpfe:** Eduard
Meier. **Derby-Schuhe:** Eduard
Meier.

Moleskin jacket: Eduard Meier.
Bespoke shirt: Gino Venturini.
Sleeveless jumper: John Crocket.
Socks: Eduard Meier. **Derby**
shoes: Eduard Meier.

Lodenjoppe: Eduard Meier.
Maßhemd: Gino Venturini. **Schal:**
Ryder & Amies. **Kordhosen:**
Brooks Taverner. **Wollstrümpfe:**
Eduard Meier. **Rauledertassel-
loafer:** Eduard Meier.

Bavarian **loden jacket:** Eduard
Meier. **Bespoke shirt:** Gino
Venturini. College **scarf:** Ryder
& Amies. Corduroy **trousers:**
Brooks Taverner. **Socks:** Eduard
Meier. Suede **tassel loafers:**
Eduard Meier.

Sakko: Jigsaw.
Hosen: Spoke.
Rauleder-Derby-
Schuhe: Loake.

Jacket: Jigsaw.
Trousers: Spoke.
Suede **Derby shoes:** Loake.

DAVID
EVANS 95

Jacke: Vintage. **Hosen:**
E. Marinella Denim. **Polohemd:**
Lacoste. **Stiefel:** Herring Shoes.
Tasche: Kjøre Projekt.

Jacket: Vintage. **Trousers:**
E. Marinella Denim. **Polo shirt:**
Lacoste. **Boots:** Herring Shoes.
Bag: Kjøre Projekt.

NICOLA
RADANO

Rollbarer Reisehut: Herbert Johnson. **Kaschmirschal:** Dante. **Tweedjacke** nach Maß: Tobias Tailors. **Maßhemd:** Emmanuele Maffeis. **Wachsjacke:** Barbour. **Maßhosen** aus Kavallerietwill: Tobias Tailors. **Chukkaboots:** Crockett & Jones.

Travel hat: Herbert Johnson. Cashmere **scarf:** Dante. Bespoke **tweed jacket:** Tobias Tailors. Made-to-measure **shirt:** Emmanuele Maffeis. Waxed cotton **jacket:** Barbour. **Bespoke** cavalry twill **trousers:** Tobias Tailors. **Chukka boots:** Crockett & Jones.

BERNHARD ROETZEL

Handgemachte **Maßjacke:**
Vaatturiliike Sauma. **Baumwoll-**
hosen: Paoloni. **Hemd:** Berg &
Berg OCBD. **Krawatte:** Viola
Milano. **Einstecktuch:** Drake's
London. **Gürtel:** Berg & Berg.
Rauleder-Loafer: Septième
Largeur. **Aktentasche:** Mismo
MS Soft Work canvas.

Handmade **made-to-measure**
jacket: Vaatturiliike Sauma.
Cotton **trousers:** Paoloni. **Shirt:**
Berg & Berg OCBD. **Tie:** Viola
Milano. **Pocket square:** Drake's
London. **Belt:** Berg & Berg
Suede loafers: Septième Largeur.
Briefcase: Mismo MS Soft Work
canvas.

Baumwollblazer: Tagliatore.
Maßhemd: Gino Venturini.
Seidenstrickkrawatte: Polo
Ralph Lauren. **Einstecktuch:**
Barba Napoli. **Hosen:** Wrangler.
Brogues: Eduard Meier.

Cotton **blazer:** Tagliatore.
Bespoke shirt: Gino Venturini.
Knitted **silk tie:** Polo Ralph
Lauren. Linen **pocket square:**
Barba Napoli. **Trousers:** Wrangler.
Brogues: Eduard Meier.

BERNHARD
ROETZEL 99

Tweedjacke mit Blasebalg-taschen und Action-back: Eduard Meier. **Maßhemd**: Emmanuele Maffeis. **Wollbinder:** Cordings of Piccadilly. **Cavalrytwillhosen** nach Maß: Tobias Tailors of Savile Row. **Wollstrümpfe:** Eduard Meier. **Derby-Schuhe:** Eduard Meier.

Tweed jacket: Eduard Meier. **Made-to-measure shirt:** Emmanuele Maffeis. Wool **tie:** Cordings of Piccadilly. **Bespoke** cavalry twill **trousers:** Tobias Tailors of Savile Row. **Socks:** Eduard Meier. **Derby shoes:** Eduard Meier.

BERNHARD
ROETZEL

Tweedjacke nach Maß: Schneider aus Florenz. **Maßhosen:** Schneider aus Florenz. **Pullover** aus Merinowolle: Italienische Marke. **Seideneinstecktuch:** Eigenes Design, Made in Italy. Ungefütterte Peccary-**Handschuhe:** Mazzoleni. **Kaschmirschal:** Begg. **Norweger nach Maß:** Jan Kielman.

Bespoke tweed jacket: Tailor from Florence. **Bespoke trousers:** Tailor from Florence. Merino wool crewneck **sweater:** Italian origin. Silk **pocket square:** Own design, made in Italy. Unlined peccary **gloves:** Mazzoleni. Cashmere **scarf:** Begg. **Bespoke Norwegian** split-toe **shoes:** Jan Kielman.

Tweedsakko nach Maß: John Coggin. **Maßhemd:** Gino Venturini. **Krawatte:** Ascot. **Kordhosen:** Cordings of Piccadilly. **Wollstrümpfe:** Sorley Socks **Rauledertasselloafer:** Eduard Meier.

Bespoke **tweed jacket:** John Coggin. **Bespoke shirt:** Gino Venturini. **Tie:** Ascot. **Corduroys:** Cordings of Piccadilly. **Socks:** Sorley Socks. Suede **tassel loafers:** Eduard Meier.

Tweedsakko: Vintage von Clark Salem. **Hemd:** Fort Belvedere. **Manschettenknöpfe:** Fort Belvedere. **Seidenstrickkrawatte:** Fort Belvedere. **Einstecktuch** mit handrollierter Kante: Polo Ralph Lauren. **Samtweste** nach Maß: Mytailor.com. **Taschenuhr:** Gruen Verithin. **Uhrenkette:** Gold, vintage. **Ring:** Gold mit Turmalin. **Baumwollhosen** nach Maß: Kiito bespoke tailor. **Chukkaboots:** St. Crispin's.

Tweed jacket: Vintage by Clark Salem. **Shirt:** Fort Belvedere. **Cufflinks:** Fort Belvedere. Knitted silk **tie:** Fort Belvedere. **Pocket square** with hand rolled edges: Polo Ralph Lauren Made-to-measure velvet **waistcoat:** Mytailor.com. **Pocket watch:** Gruen Verithin. Gold **watch chain:** vintage. **Pinky ring:** Gold with Turmalin. Bespoke cotton drill **trousers:** Kiito bespoke tailor. **Chukka boots:** St. Crispin's.

Maßsakko: Olego Tailoring.
Hemd: Mangas. **Kawatte:**
Massimo Dutti. **Einstecktuch:**
Cencibel. **Hosen:** Gant.
Strümpfe: Urban. **Rauleder-
Oxfords:** Vass Shoes.

Bespoke jacket: Olego Tailoring.
Shirt: Mangas. **Tie:** Massimo
Dutti. **Pocket square:** Cencibel.
Trousers: Gant. **Socks:** Urban.
Suede **oxfords:** Vass Shoes.

104 ✕ **DAVID GARCÍA
BRAGADO**

Leinensakko nach Maß: Sartoria
Langa. **Maßhemd:** Luca Avitabile.
Krawatte: Shibumi Berlin.
Seideneinstecktuch: Rubinacci.
Gabardinehosen nach Maß:
Anderson & Sheppard.
Brogues: Stefano Bemer.

Bespoke linen **jacket:** Sartoria
Langa. **Bespoke shirt:** Luca
Avitabile. **Tie:** Shibumi Berlin.
Silk **pocket square:** Rubinacci.
Bespoke gabardine **trousers:**
Anderson & Sheppard.
Brogues: Stefano Bemer.

Maßsakko: Sastrería Serna.
Maßhemd: Sastrería Langa.
Maßhosen: Sastrería Langa.
Hosenträger: Sastrería
Haberdashers. **Wolleinstecktuch:**
Rushmore. Einzeln angefertigte
Pennyloafer: Vidal Fernández.

Bespoke jacket: Sastrería Serna.
Bespoke shirt: Sastrería Langa.
Made-to-measure **trousers:**
Sastrería Langa. **Braces:** Sastrería
Haberdashers. Wool **pocket
square:** Rushmore. Made-to-order
Penny loafers: Vidal Fernández.

Maßsakko: Sartoria Ciardi.
Maßhosen: Sartoria Caracciolo.
Polohemd: Lacoste. **Tassel-**
Loafer: Herring Shoes.

Bespoke jacket: Sartoria Ciardi.
Bespoke trousers: Sartoria
Caracciolo. **Polo shirt:** Lacoste.
Tassel loafers: Herring Shoes.

NICOLA
RADANO

Hosen: Tommy Hilfiger.
Maßhemd: Basanta Tailoring.
Gürtel: Meermin. **Loafer:**
Meermin.

Trousers: Tommy Hilfiger. **Made-to-measure shirt:** Basanta
Tailoring. **Belt:** Meermin.
Loafers: Meermin.

**DAVID GARCIA
BRAGADO** 109

ANLASS KLEIDUNG

Anzüge für förmliche Anlässe sind Frack, Cut, Smoking und das weiße Dinnerjacket. Frack und Cut sind die ältesten Modellformen und zugleich die vornehmsten. Der Frack wird grundsätzlich nur am Abend getragen, der Cut, der auf Englisch auch »morning coat« heißt, nur am Tage. Der Smoking hat sich in den 1920ern als bequemere und etwas weniger steife Alternative zum Frack durchgesetzt. Zum Smoking trägt der Herr stets eine schwarze Schleife, zum Frack eine weiße. Zu den Schoßröcken, also Cut und Frack, wird der Zylinder getragen. Zum Smoking der Bowler oder ein Homburger. Wer mag, leistet sich auch noch einen Abendmantel, der Gabardinemantel tut es aber auch.

FORMAL WEAR

Tailcoat, morning coat, dinner suit, and white dinner jacket—these are the outfits worn for special, formal occasions. Tailcoat and morning coat are the oldest models, and they are also the most elegant. A tailcoat is only ever worn at night; the morning coat is only worn during the day. The dinner suit, which is called Tuxedo in the US, was first introduced in the 1920ies as the more comfortable and slightly less rigid alternative to the tailcoat. Gentlemen always wear a black bowtie with their dinner suit, and always a white bowtie with their tailcoat. A top hat is worn with the tailcoat and cut; a bowler hat or homburg hat will add the finishing touch to your dinner suit. If you wish, you can top off everything with an evening coat, but a gabardine coat will serve the purpose just as well.

Samtsmokingjacke: Maßanfertigung aus Chicago von 1940. **Smokinghose** in Mitternachtsblau: Maßanfertigung aus Chicago von 1940. **Smokinghemd:** Vintage von Brooks Brothers. **Schleife** zum Selberbinden aus Failleseide: Fort Belvedere. **Leineneinstecktuch:** Fort Belvedere. **Ring** am kleinen Finger: Achteckiger Heliotrop mit 14 Karat Gelbgold. Steckknöpfe und **Manschettenknöpfe:** 14 Karat mit Platin und Abalone. **Seidenstrümpfe:** Fort Belvedere. **Abendschuhe** mit Seidenschleifen: Prototype für Fort Belvedere.

Velvet **smoking jacket:** Bespoke tailored in 1940 in Chicago. Midnight blue **trousers:** Bespoke tailored in 1940 in Chicago. **Dinner shirt:** Vintage by Brooks Brothers. Silk Faille **bow tie:** Fort Belvedere. **Linen pocket square:** Fort Belvedere. **Pinky Ring:** Octagonal Bloodstone with 14k yellow gold, vintage. **Dress set:** cufflinks and studs 14k with Platinum and Abalone. Silk **socks:** Fort Belvedere. **Court shoes:** Prototypes for Fort Belvedere.

SVEN RAPHAEL SCHNEIDER

Cut nach Maß: Vintage von Jureit.
Leinenweste: Pakeman Catto
Carter. **Hosen:** Hackett. **Maßhemd:**
Emanuel Berg. **Krawatte:** Hermès
Einstecktuch: Barba Napoli.
Zylinder: Christy's. **Stockschirm:**
Deutsches Fabrikat aus den
1950ern. **Oxfords:** Eduard Meier.

Bespoke cutaway **coat:** Vintage,
Jureit. Linen **waistcoat:** Pakeman
Catto Carter. **Trousers:** Hackett.
Made-to-measure shirt: Emanuel
Berg. **Tie:** Hermes. **Pocket square:**
Barba Napoli. **Top hat:** Christy's.
Umbrella: German make from the
1950s. **Oxfords:** Eduard Meier.

Abendanzug: Vintage von Ströms. **Smokinghemd** nach Maß: Shirtonomy. **Lackschuhe:** Vom Vater, Marke unbekannt.

Dinner suit: Vintage by Ströms. **Made-to-measure dinner shirt:** Shirtonomy. **Patent leather shoes:** His father's old shoes, brand unknown.

114 X ERIK MANNBY

Maßanzug: Michele Mescia.
Hemd: Camiceria Artigiana
Carmen. **Wollkrawatte nach
Maß:** Krawattenmacher aus
Neapel. **Seideneinstecktuch:**
Eigenes Design, italienische
Fertigung. **Oxfords nach Maß:**
Jan Kielman.

Bespoke suit: Michele Mescia.
Shirt: Camiceria Artigiana Carmen.
Made-to-measure wool **tie:**
Neapolitan tiemaker. Silk
pocket square: Own design,
made in Italy. **Bespoke oxfords:**
Jan Kielman.

TORSTEN
GRUNWALD

Smoking: Tobias Tailors of Savile Row. **Smokinghemd** nach Maß: Emanuel Berg. **Schleife:** Charvet. **Einstecktuch:** Barba Napoli. **Plaintip-Oxfords** mit Satin-schnürbändern: Eduard Meier. **Bowler:** Lock & Co.

Dinner suit: Tobias Tailors of Savile Row. Made-to-measure **dinner shirt:** Emanuel Berg. **Bow tie:** Charvet. **Pocket square:** Barba Napoli. **Plain toe oxfords** with Satin laces: Eduard Meier. **Bowler:** Lock & Co.

BERNHARD ROETZEL

Abendanzug: Knack Men.
Lackschuhe: Meermin.
Schmuck aus Silber und Jade:
Susi Gesto Master artisan
goldsmith.

Dinner suit: Knack Men.
Patent leather shoes: Meermin.
Jewelry in silver and jade: Susi
Gesto Master artisan goldsmith.

**DAVID GARCÍA
BRAGADO** ✕ **117**

Abendanzug nach Maß: Cesare Attolini. **Smokinghemd** nach Maß aus irischem Leinen: Cesare Attolini. **Schleife** aus Seidenripps: Cesare Attolini. **Einstecktuch** aus irischem Leinen: Simonnot Godard. **Abendschuhe** aus Kalbsleder: St. Crispin's. **Abendumhang:** Venezianischer Tabarro von Tabarrificio Veneto.

Bespoke dinner suit: Cesare Attolini. **Bespoke** Irish linen **dinner shirt:** Cesare Attolini. Grosgrain **bow tie:** Cesare Attolini. Irish linen **pocket square:** Simonnot Godard. Calfskin court **shoes:** St. Crispin's. **Cape:** Venetian Tabarro by Tabarrificio Veneto.

Mitternachtsblauer **Abendanzug:** Maßanfertigung aus Chicago von 1940. **Smokinghemd:** Vintage von Brooks Brothers. **Schleife** aus Failleseide: Fort Belvedere. **Leineneinstecktuch:** Fort Belvedere. **Ring:** Achteckiger Heliotrop mit 14 Karat Gelbgold. **Steckknöpfe und Manschettenknöpfe:** 14 Karat mit Platin und Abalone **Seidenstrümpfe:** Fort Belvedere. **Lacklederoxfords:** Fort Belvedere. Breite **Abendschnürbänder:** Fort Belvedere.

Midnight blue **dinner suit:** bespoke tailored in 1940 in Chicago. **Dinnershirt:** Vintage by Brooks Brothers. Silk Faille **bow tie:** Fort Belvedere. Linen **pocket square:** Fort Belvedere. **Pinky Ring:** Octagonal Bloodstone with 14k yellow gold, vintage. **Dress set:** cufflinks and studs 14k with Platinum and Abalone. Silk **socks:** Fort Belvedere. **Patent Leather oxfords:** Fort Belvedere. Wide evening **shoelaces:** Fort Belvedere.

Smoking: Ralph Lauren.
Maßhemd: Fralbo. **Schleife:**
Rubinacci. **Seideneinstecktuch:**
Serà. **Manschettenknöpfe:**
Vintage. **Uhr:** Vintage gold
Longines Quartz. **Lackschuhe:**
Barrett.

Tuxedo: Ralph Lauren. **Bespoke
shirt:** Fralbo. **Bow tie:** Rubinacci.
Silk **pocket square:** Serà.
Cufflinks: Vintage. **Watch:**
Vintage gold Longines Quartz.
Patent leather shoes: Barrett.

**GIORGIO
GIANGIULIO**

Frack nach Maß mit Hosen
und Weste: Vom Großvater.
Lackschuhe: Vom Großvater.

Bespoke tailcoat with trousers
and waistcoat: Grandfather's.
Patent leather shoes:
Grandfather's.

ERIK
MANNBY ✕ 121

ANHANG

APPENDIX

Die Gäste in alphabetischer Reihenfolge/ The guests in alphabetical order

Ich bedanke mich bei allen, die zu diesem Buch beigetragen haben./ I would like to thank everybody who has contributed to this book.

Bernhard Roetzel

Autor und Journalist/ Author and journalist
www.bernhardroetzel.de
www.facebook.com/ gentlemanbernhardroetzel
Instagram: bernhardroetzel
www.ullmannmedien. com/authors/ bernhard-roetzel/

David Garcia Bragado
Gründer und Chef-Redakteur/
Founder and Editor-in-Chief
www.vestirseporlospies.es

Stéphane Butticé
Gründer und Redakteur von/
Founder and Editor of
www.gentlemanchemistry.com
Holland&Sherry France
(Verkauf/Sales)
Instagram: gentlemanchemistry

Simon Crompton
Gründer von Permanent Style/
Founder of Permanent Style
www.simoncrompton.co.uk
www.permanentstyle.co.uk

David Evans
Grey Fox Blog
www.greyfoxblog.com
Instagram: GreyFoxBlog

Giorgio Giangiulio
Gründer und Redakteur/
Founder and Editor of
www.giorgiogiangiulio.com
Instagram: giorgiogiangiulio

Salvador Godoy
Gründer und Redakteur von/
Founder and Editor of
www.sinabrochar.com

Gründer und Partner von/
Founder and Editor of
www.tadinostore.es

Torsten Grunwald
Gründer und Chefredakteur von/
Founder and Editor-in-Chief of
www.sartorialnotes.com
www.denvelklaedtemand.dk

Wolfgang Hölker
Verleger/Publisher
www.coppenrath.de

Michael Jondral
Inhaber von/ Owner of
Michael Jondral
www.michaeljondral.com
Instagram: michaeljondral

Erik Mannby
Mitbegründer von/Co-founder of
www.e-f-v.com
Redakteur bei/Editor at
sowhatelseisnew.tumblr.com
Redakteur und Mitgründer von/
Co-founder and Editor of
www.svenskaherrar.se

Peter Eduard Meier
Inhaber Ältestes Deutsches
Schuhhaus/Owner of Germany's
oldest shoe shop Eduard Meier,
www.edmeier.de

Olof Nithenius
Stil- und Modejournalist/Freelance
style and fashion writer
Freier Redakteur/Contributing editor
www.manolo.se and
Plaza Uomo Magazine
Instagram: olof1982

Nicola Radano
Gründer und Redakteur von/
Founder and Editor of
Me, Myself & I
www.nicolaradano.com
Gründer von/Founder of
Spacca Neapolis Ties

Juho Rehakka
Gründer von/Founder of
The Nordic Fit
www.thenordicfit.com
Instagram: thenordicfit

Sven Raphael Schneider
Gründer von/ Founder of
Gentleman's Gazette und
Fort Belvedere.
www.gentlemansgazette.com
www.fortbelvedere.com

Andreas Weinås
Redakteur bei/ Editor of
www.manolo.se
Instagram: andreasweinas

Hersteller und Lieferanten der abgebildeten Kleidungsstücke, Schuhe und Accessoires in alphabetischer Reihenfolge./Makers and suppliers of the presented garments, shoes and accessories in alphabetical order.

Herrenschneider und Maßkonfektion/ Bespoke Tailors and Made-To-Measure clothes

A. Caraceni
Anderson & Sheppard
Basanta Tailoring
Belvest
B&Tailor
Canovas Club
Cesare Attolini
Cove & Co
d' Avenza
Duran Tailoring
Eduardo De Simone
E-F-V
Fields Tailoring
John Coggin
Kathrin Emmer
Kiito bespoke tailor
Langa Tailoring
Marco Cerrato Napoli
Michael Possanner
Michele Mescia
Mr Johnsons Wardrobe
Mytailor.com
Olego Tailoring
Purwin & Radczun
Sastrería TomBlack
Sastrería Serna
Sartoria Caliendo
Sartoria Caracciolo
Sartoria CorCos
Sartoria Ciardi

Sartoria Crimi
Sartoria Diletto
Sartoria Langa
Sartoria Peluso
Sartoria Ripense
Sartoria Sodano
Sartoria Solito
Sastrería Haberdashers
Sastrería 91
Serna Tailoring
Tailor 4 Less
Tobias Tailors of Savile Row
Urban Tailoring
Vaatturiliike Sauma
Volkmar Arnulf
Zaremba Bespoke

Hemden/Shirts

Barba Napoli
Berg & Berg
Brooks Brothers
Camiceria Artigiana Carmen
Charvet
Daniels & Korff
Emanuel Berg
Emmanuele Maffeis
Eton
Finamore 1925
Fort Belvedere
Francesco Merolla
Frank Foster
Fralbo
Gino Venturini
Harvie & Hudson
Luca Avitabile

Luxire
Mangas
New & Lingwood
Pedro del Hierro
Sangar
Sastrería Langa
Sastrería Sánchez-Caro
Shirtonomy
Siniscalchi
Sonrisa
Turnbull & Asser
Urban Tailoring
Vanacore
Vaatturiliike Sauma

Krawatten und Einstecktücher/ Ties and pocket squares

Ascot Karl Moese
Berg & Berg
Blick Ties
Calabrese 1924
Cencibel
Charvet
Drake's London
E. Marinella
Exquisite Trimmings
Harvie & Hudson
Hermès
Herrainpukimo
H. N. White
John Comfort
Kapital
Kent Wang

Louise and Zaid
Mattabisch
Nicky Milano
R Culturi
Rampley & Co
Robert Talbott
Rushmore
Rubinacci
Serà
Shibumi Berlin
Simonnot Godard
Spacca Neapolis Ties
Striessnig
TadinoStore
The Gentleman
Vanda Fine Clothing
Wilh. Jungmann & Neffe
Viola Milano

Herrenausstatter und Konfektionäre/ Gentleman's Outfitters and Suit Manufacturers

American Apparel
Baron & Earl
Braun Hamburg
Breuer
Boglioli
Brooks Taverner
Chad Prom
Chelsea Farmer's Club
Cordings of Piccadilly
Cortefiel
Daniels & Korff
Eduard Meier

El Corte Inglés
Gabo Napoli
Gant
Hackett
Harry Stedman
Jigsaw
J. Keydge
Knack Men
Ladage & Oelke
Lacoste
Land's End
Levi's
Luxire
Manolo x Ströms
Massimo Dutti
Oscar Jacobson
Pakeman Catto Carter
Paoloni
Paul Stuart
Ralph Lauren
Ring Jacket
Spoke
Stewart
Stòffa
Ströms
Tabarrificio Veneto
Tagliatore
Tommy Hilfiger
Wrangler

Strickwaren/Knitwear
Alan Paine
Berg & Berg
John Crocket
John Laing for Al Bazar
Milano
J. Lindeberg
Saman Amel

Uniqlo
William Lockie

**Mäntel und
Wetterschutz/
Overcoats and
weather wear**
Chrysalis
Eduard Meier
Grenfell für Ladage & Oelke
Lardini
Mackintosh

Schuhe/Shoes
Alfred Sargent
Allen-Edmonds
Antica Cuoieria Firenze
Barre & Brunel Footwear
Barrett
Beretta
Benjamin Klemann
Carmina
Church's
CQP SNEAKERS
Crockett & Jones
Eduard Meier
Edward Green
Edward's
George Cleverley
G. H. Bass
Herring Shoes
Jan Kielman
John Lobb
Larson & Jehan
Loake
Lottusse
Saint Crispin's
Scarosso

Septième Largeur
Shoepassion
Stefano Bemer
Tadeusz Januszkiewicz
Trickers
Red Wing
Lazo y Duque
László Vass
Valverde del Camino
Vickermann & Stoya
Vidal Fernandez
Wildsmith
Yanko

**Strümpfe, Kopfbede-
ckungen, Accessoires,
Sonnenbrillen, Taschen
und Gepäck/
Socks, headwear,
accessories, sunglasses,
bags and lugagge**
Absolute Bretón
Albert Thurston
Akah Lederwaren
Ascione Napoli
Begg
Borsalino
Bresciani
Brixton
Christy's
Dante
Di Carlo
Drake's
Falke
Fox Umbrellas
Frank Clegg
Glenroyal
Hans Øster

Hartmann Luggage
Herbert Johnson
James Lock
James Smith & Sons
KjØre Projekt
Lafont
Lock & Co
Linjer
Maglia
Mazzoleni
Meier Bruecher
Meermin
Miler Menswear
Mismo
Oliver Peoples
Persol
Roeckl
Ryder & Amies
Sorley Socks
Sozzi Milano
Susi Gesto Master
  artisan goldsmith
The Armoury
Thomas Riemer
Von Jungfeld

Uhren/Watches
Festina
Gruen Verithin
Tudor
Waltham